ARDUINO NEW DIFFERENT PROJECTS TACHOMETER UTILIZING, ADVANCED CODE LOCK, SHADING DETECTOR, ELECTRONIC VOTING MACHINE, BIDIRECTIONAL VIS-ITOR COUNTER ETC..,

CONTENTS

ACKNOWLEDGMENTS

The writer might want to recognize the diligent work of the article group in assembling this book. He might likewise want to recognize the diligent work of the Raspberry Pi Foundation and the Arduino bunch for assembling items and networks that help to make the Internet of Things increasingly open to the overall population. Yahoo for the democratization of innovation!

INTRODUCTION

The Internet of Things (IOT) is a perplexing idea comprised of numerous PCs and numerous correspondence ways. Some IOT gadgets are associated with the Internet and some are most certainly not. Some IOT gadgets structure swarms that convey among themselves. Some are intended for a solitary reason, while some are increasingly universally useful PCs. This book is intended to demonstrate to you the IOT from the back to front. By structure IOT gadgets, the per user will comprehend the essential ideas and will almost certainly develop utilizing the rudiments to make his or her very own IOT applications. These included ventures will tell the per user the best way to assemble their very own IOT ventures and to develop the models appeared. The significance of Computer Security in IOT gadgets is additionally talked about and different systems for protecting the IOT from unapproved clients or programmers. The most significant takeaway from this book is in structure the tasks yourself.

1. WORKING OF FORCE SENSOR WITH ARDUINO

In this venture we will build up a fun circuit utilizing Force sensor and Arduino Uno. This circuit produces sound directly identified with power applied on the sensor. For that we are going to interface FORCE sensor with Arduino Uno. In UNO, we are going utilize 8 piece ADC (Analog to Digital Conversion) highlight to carry out the responsibility.

Force Sensor or Force Sensitive Resistor

A FORCE sensor is a transducer which changes its opposition when weight is applied on surface. Power sensor is accessible in various sizes and shapes. We are gonna to utilize one of the less expensive adaptations since we needn't bother with a lot of precision here. FSR400 is the least expensive power sensors in the market. The image of FSR400 is appeared in underneath figure. They are likewise called Force-touchy resistor or FSR as its obstruction changes as per the power or weight applied to it. At the point when weight is applied to this power detecting resistor its obstruction diminishes that is, the opposition is conversely relative to the power applied. So when no weight is applied on it, the obstruction of FSR will be exceptionally high.

Presently note that the FSR 400 is delicate along the length, the power or weight ought to be focused on the labyrinth on the center of eye of sensor, as appeared in figure. In the event that the power is applied at wrong occasions the gadget could harm forever.

Another significant thing to realize that, the sensor can drive flows of high extend. So remember the driving flows while introducing. Additionally the sensor has a breaking point on power that is 10 Newtons. So we can apply just 1Kg of weight. On the off chance that loads higher than 1Kg applied the sensor may give a few deviations. On the off chance that it's expanded more than 3Kg. the sensor may harm for all time.

As advised before this sensor is utilized to detect the adjustments in pressure. So when the weight is applied over FORCE sensor, the opposition is changed definitely. The obstruction of FS400 over weight is appeared in beneath chart,

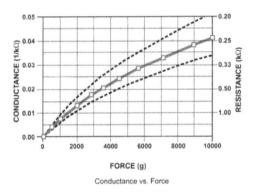

FORCE (g)

Conductance vs. Force

As appeared in above figure, the obstruction between the two contacts of sensor diminishes with weight or the conductance among two contacts of sensor increments. The obstruction of an unadulterated conductor is given by:

$$R = \frac{\rho l}{A}$$

Where,

p-Resistivity of conductor

l= Length of conductor

A= Area of conductor.
Presently consider a conductor with obstruction "R", if some weight is applied over conductor, the region on conductor diminishes and the length of conductor increments because of weight. So by equation the opposition of conductor should increment, as the obstruction R is contrarily relative to territory and furthermore legitimately corresponding to length l.

So with this for a conductor under strain or weight the opposition of conductor increments. Be that as it may, this change is little contrasted with generally opposition. For an extensive change numerous conductors are stacked together. This is the thing that occurs inside the Force Sensors appeared in above figure. On looking carefully one can sees numerous lines inside the sensor. Every one of these lines speaks to a conductor. Affectability of sensor is in conductor numbers.

Be that as it may, for this situation the obstruction will diminish with pressure in light of the fact that the material utilized here is certifiably not an unadulterated conductor. The FSR here are strong polymer thick film (PTF) gadgets. So these are not unadulterated conductor material gadgets. These are comprised of a material, that display a decline in obstruction with increment in power applied to the outside of the sensor. This material shows qualities as appeared in chart of FSR.

This adjustment in obstruction can do nothing more than a bad memory except if we can understand them. The current controller can just peruse the odds in voltage and nothing less, for this we are going to utilize voltage divider circuit, with that we can determine the obstruction change as voltage change.

Voltage divider is a resistive circuit and is appeared in figure. In this resistive system we have one consistent obstruction and other variable opposition. As appeared in figure, R1 here is a consistent opposition and R2 is FORCE sensor which goes about as an obstruction. The midpoint of branch is taken to estimation. With R2 change, we have change at Vout. So with this we have a voltage change with weight.

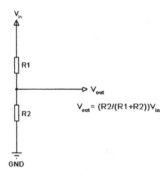

$$V_{out} = (R2/(R1+R2))V_{in}$$

Presently significant thing to note here is, the information taken by the controller for ADC transformation is as low as 50µAmp. This stacking impact of opposition based voltage divider is significant as the current drawn from Vout of voltage divider builds the mistake rate increments, for the present we need not stress over stacking impact.

The most effective method to check a FSR Sensor

The power detecting resistor can be tried utilizing a multimeter. Interface the 2 pins of FSR sensor to the multimeter without applying any power and check the obstruction esteem, it will be high. At that point apply some power to its surface and see the decrement in obstruction esteem.

Utilizations of FSR Sensor

Power detecting resistors are for the most part used to make pressure-detecting "catches". They are utilized in an assortment of fields, for example, vehicle inhabitance sensors, resistive touch-cushions, automated fingertips, counterfeit appendages, keypads, Foot pronation frameworks, melodic instruments, Embedded Electronics, Testing and Measurement Equipment, OEM Development Kit and versatile gadgets, sports. They are utilized in Augmented Reality frameworks just as to upgrade versatile communication.

Components Required

Equipment: Arduino Uno, 1000 uF Capacitor, Power supply (5v), 100K? resistor, 100nF capacitor (3 pieces), Buzzer, FSR400 Force sensor, 220? resistor.

Programming: Atmel studio 6.2 or Aurdino daily

Circuit Diagram and Working Explanation

The circuit association for interfacing Force detecting Resistor with Arduino is appeared in underneath graph.

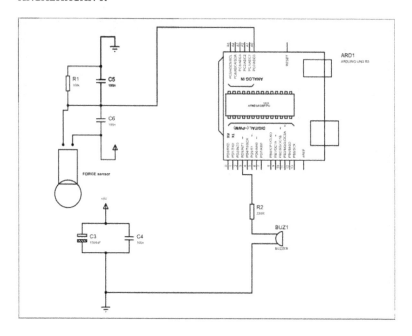

The voltage crosswise over sensor isn't totally direct; it will be a boisterous one. To sift through the clamor a capacitors are put over every resistor in the divider circuit as appeared in figure.

Here we are going to take the voltage gave by the divider (voltage which speaks to weight directly) and feed it into one of ADC channels of UNO. After transformation we are going to take that advanced worth (speaking to weight) and relate it to PWM esteem for driving the bell.

So with weight we have a PWM esteem which changes its obligation proportion contingent upon advanced worth. Higher the computerized worth higher the obligation proportion of PWM so higher the commotion created by ringer. So we related load to sound.

Before going any further lets talk about Analog to Digital Conversion of Arduino Uno. ARDUINO has 6 Analog to Digital Conversion channels, as show in figure. In those any one or every one of them can be utilized as contributions for simple voltage. The UNO ADC is of 10 piece goals (so the number qualities from $(0-(2^10)$ 1023)).This implies that it will guide input voltages somewhere in the range of 0 and 5 volts into whole number qualities somewhere in the range of 0 and 1023. So for each $(5/1024 = 4.9mV)$ / unit.

Here we are gonna to utilize A0 of UNO.

We have to know scarcely any things.

1. analogRead(pin);
2. analogReference();
3. analogReadResolution(bits);

As a matter of first importance the UNO ADC channels has a default reference estimation of 5V. This implies we can give a most extreme info voltage of 5V for ADC transformation at any information channel. Since certain sensors give voltages from 0-2.5V, with a 5V reference we get lesser exactness, so we have a guidance that empowers us to change this reference esteem. So for changing the reference esteem we have ("analogReference();") For now we leave it as.

As default we get the most extreme board ADC goals which is 10bits, this goals can be changed by utilizing guidance ("analogReadResolution(bits);"). This goals change can prove to be useful for certain cases. Until further notice we leave it as.

Presently if the above conditions are set to default, the we can peruse an incentive from ADC of channel '0' by straightforwardly calling capacity "analogRead(pin);", here "stick" speaks to stick where we associated simple sign, for this situation it would be "A0". The incentive from ADC can be taken into a number as "int SENSOR-VALUE = analogRead(A0); ", by this guidance the incentive after ADC gets put away in the whole number "SEN-SORVALUE".

The PWM of Arduino Uno can accomplished at any of pins symbolized as " ~ " on the PCB board. There are six PWM directs in UNO. We are gonna to utilize PIN3 for our motivation.

analogWrite(3,VALUE);

From above condition we can legitimately get the PWM signal at the comparing pin. The first parameter in quite a while is for picking the stick number of PWM signal. Second parameter is for composing obligation proportion.

The PWM estimation of UNO can be changed from 0 to 255. With "0" as most minimal to "255" as most noteworthy. With 255 as obligation proportion we will get 5V at PIN3. On the off chance that the obligation proportion is given as 125 we will get 2.5V at PIN3.

Presently we have 0-1024 incentive as ADC yield and 0-255 as PWM obligation proportion. So ADC is around multiple times the PWM proportion. So by partitioned the ADC result by 4 we will get the surmised obligation proportion.

With that we will have a PWM signal whose obligation proportion changes directly with weight. This being given to ringer, we have sound generator relying upon weight.

Code
```
int sensorvalue =0; // Interger for storing ADC result
void setup()
{
     pinMode(A0,INPUT); // ADC result input
     pinMode(3,OUTPUT); // PWM signal output pin
}
void loop()
{
        sensorvalue = analogRead(A0); // Read analog
value and store it in integer
```

```
    analogWrite(3,sensorvalue/4); // PWM duty ratio
given
}
```

◆ ◆ ◆

2. PROGRAMMED WATER LEVEL INDICATOR AS WELL AS CONTROLLER UTILIZING ARDUINO

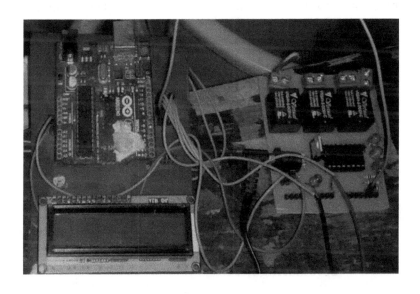

In this Arduino based programmed water level pointer and controller venture we are gonna to gauge the water level by utilizing ultrasonic sensors. Fundamental head of ultrasonic division estimation relies upon REVERBERATION. Right when sound waves are transmitted in condition at that point they return back to the beginning as ECHO as a result of striking on any obstruction. So we need to just ascertain its voyaging time of the two sounds means active time and returning time to inception in the wake of striking on any hindrance. What's progressively, after a few estimation we can get an outcome that is the separation. This idea is used in our water controller venture where the water engine siphon is normally turned on when water level in the tank ends up being low. You can likewise check this basic water level pointer circuit for a less difficult adaptation of this venture.

Components

- Arduino Uno
- Ultrasonic sensor Module
- 16x2 LCD
- Relay 6 Volt
- ULN2003
- 7806
- PVT
- Copper wire
- 9 volt battery or 12 Voltadaptor
- Connecting wires

Ultrasonic Sensor Module

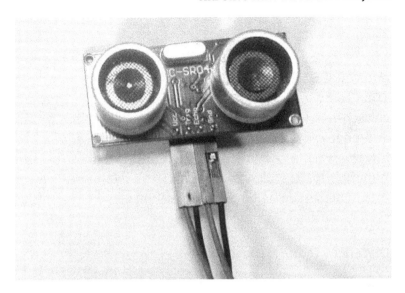

Ultrasonic sensor HC-SR04 is used to quantify separation in scope of 2cm-400cm with exactness of 3mm. The sensor module comprises of ultrasonic transmitter, collector and the control circuit.

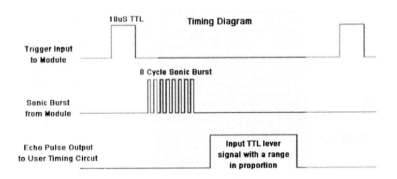

The ultrasonic sensor module deals with the normal marvel of ECHO of sound. A heartbeat is sent for about 10us to trigger the module. After which the module consequently sends 8 cycles of 40 KHz ultrasound sign and checks its reverberation. The sign subsequent to hitting with a snag returns back and is caught by the beneficiary. In this way the partition of the hindrance from the sensor is basically determined by the equation given as

Distance = (time x speed)/2.

Here we have partitioned the result of speed and time by 2 in light of the fact that the time is the all out time it took to arrive at the impediment and return back. Subsequently an opportunity to arrive at deterrent is simply a large portion of the absolute time taken.

Working of Automatic Water Level Controller

Working of this undertaking is very basic we have utilized Ultrasonic sensor module which sends the sound waves in the water tank and recognizes impression of sound waves that is ECHO. As a matter of first importance we needs to trigger the ultrasonic sensor module to transmit signal by utilizing Arduino and afterward stand by to get ECHO. Arduino peruses the time among activating and got ECHO. We realize that speed of sound is around 340 m/s. so we can figure separation by utilizing given recipe:

Distance= (travel time/2) * speed of sound

Where speed of sound is around 340m every second.

By utilizing this techniques we gets good ways from sensor to water surface. After it we have to figure water level.

Presently we have to ascertain the complete length of water tank. As we probably am aware the length of water tank then we can figure the water level by subtracting coming about separation originating from ultrasonic from complete length of tank. Furthermore, we will get the water level separation. Presently we can change over this water level in to the percent of water, and can show it on LCD. The working of the total water level marker task is appeared in beneath square graph.

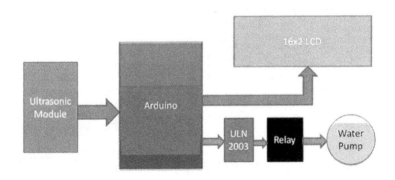

Circuit Diagram and Explanation

As appeared in the water level controller circuit given beneath, Ultrasonic sensor module's "trigger" and "reverberation" pins are straightforwardly associated with stick 10 and 11 of arduino. A 16x2 LCD is associated with arduino in 4-piece mode. Control stick RS, RW and En are legitimately associated with arduino stick 7, GND and 6. Furthermore, information stick D4-D7 is associated with 5, 4, 3 and 2 of arduino, and ringer is associated at stick 12. 6 Volt hand-off is likewise associated at stick 8 of arduino through ULN2003 for killing on or turning the water engine siphon. A voltage controller 7805 is additionally utilized for giving 5 volt to hand-off and to outstanding circuit.

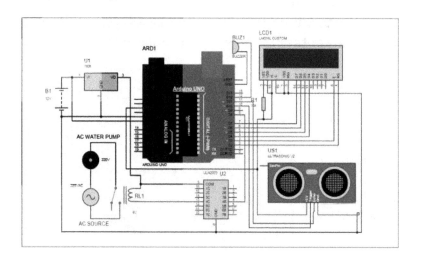

In this circuit Ultrasonic sensor module is set at the highest point of basin (water tank) for show. This sensor module will peruse the separation between sensor module and water surface, and it will show the separation on LCD screen with message "Water Space in Tank is:". It implies we are here demonstrating void spot of separation or volume for water rather than water level. Due to this usefulness we can utilize this framework in any water tank. At the point when void water level spans at separation around 30 cm then Arduino turns ON the water siphon by driving hand-off. What's more, presently LCD will show "LOW Water Level" "Engine turned ON", and Relay status LED will begin shining

Presently if the vacant space comes to at separation around 12 cm arduino turns OFF the hand-off and LCD will show "Tank is full" "Engine Turned OFF". Bell additionally blare for quite a while and hand-off status LED will killed.

Programming

To program Arduino for water level controller, first we characterize all the stick that we are going to use in the task for interfacing outer gadgets like transfer, LCD, ringer and so forth.

```
#define trigger 10

#define echo 11

#define motor 8
```

```
#define buzzer 12
```

By then we introduce all of the devices utilized in venture.

```
lcd.begin(16,2);

pinMode(trigger,OUTPUT);

pinMode(echo,INPUT);

pinMode(motor, OUTPUT);

pinMode(buzzer, OUTPUT);

lcd.print(" Water Level ");

lcd.setCursor(0,1);

lcd.print(" Indicator ");

delay(2000);
```

Presently instate the ultrasonic sensor module and read time of sending and getting time of ultrasonic waves or sound by utilizing pulseIn(pin). At that point perform figurings and show the outcome on 16x2 LCD by utilizing fitting capacities.

```
digitalWrite(trigger,HIGH);

delayMicroseconds(10);

digitalWrite(trigger,LOW);

delayMicroseconds(2);

time=pulseIn(echo,HIGH);

distance=time*340/20000;

lcd.clear();

lcd.print("Water Space In ");

lcd.setCursor(0,1);

lcd.print("Tank is: ");

lcd.print(distance);

lcd.print("Cm");
```

After it we check conditions if water tank is full or water level is LOW, and take activities appropriately.

```
if(distance<12 && temp==0)

{

    digitalWrite(motor, LOW);

    digitalWrite(buzzer, HIGH);

    lcd.clear();

    lcd.print("Water Tank Full ");

    lcd.setCursor(0,1);

    lcd.print("Motor Turned OFF");

    delay(2000);

    digitalWrite(buzzer, LOW);

    delay(3000);

    temp=1;

}

  else if(distance<12 && temp==1)
```

```
{

    digitalWrite(motor, LOW);

    lcd.clear();

    lcd.print("Water Tank Full ");

    lcd.setCursor(0,1);

    lcd.print("Motor Turned OFF");

    delay(5000);

}
```

Code

```
#include <LiquidCrystal.h>

#define trigger 10
#define echo 11
#define motor 8
#define buzzer 12

LiquidCrystal lcd(7,6,5,4,3,2);

float time=0,distance=0;
int temp=0;
```

ANBAZHAGAN K

```
void setup()
{
lcd.begin(16,2);
pinMode(trigger,OUTPUT);
pinMode(echo,INPUT);
pinMode(motor, OUTPUT);
pinMode(buzzer, OUTPUT);
lcd.print(" Water Level ");
lcd.setCursor(0,1);
lcd.print(" Indicator ");
delay(2000);
}


void loop()
{
lcd.clear();
digitalWrite(trigger,LOW);
delayMicroseconds(2);
digitalWrite(trigger,HIGH);
delayMicroseconds(10);
digitalWrite(trigger,LOW);
delayMicroseconds(2);
time=pulseIn(echo,HIGH);
distance=time*340/20000;
lcd.clear();
lcd.print("Water Space In ");
lcd.setCursor(0,1);
lcd.print("Tank is: ");
lcd.print(distance);
lcd.print("Cm");
```

```
delay(2000);
if(distance<12 && temp==0)
{
  digitalWrite(motor, LOW);
  digitalWrite(buzzer, HIGH);
  lcd.clear();
  lcd.print("Water Tank Full ");
  lcd.setCursor(0,1);
  lcd.print("Motor Turned OFF");
  delay(2000);
  digitalWrite(buzzer, LOW);
  delay(3000);
  temp=1;
}


  else if(distance<12 && temp==1)
{
  digitalWrite(motor, LOW);
  lcd.clear();
  lcd.print("Water Tank Full ");
  lcd.setCursor(0,1);
  lcd.print("Motor Turned OFF");
  delay(5000);
}


  else if(distance>30)
{
  digitalWrite(motor, HIGH);
  lcd.clear();
```

```
lcd.print("LOW Water Level");
lcd.setCursor(0,1);
lcd.print("Motor Turned ON");
delay(5000);
temp=0;
}
}
```

◆ ◆ ◆

3. PC CONTROLLED HOME AUTOMATION UTILIZING ARDUINO

This undertaking clarifies planning a home computerization framework which is constrained by a PC to turn On and switch Off different electrical and hardware gadgets. For exhibition we have utilized 3 zero watt bulbs which shows LIGHT, FAN and TV. It utilizes Arduino Uno board as a controller and a 5V transfer to interface lights with the circuit.

There could be different sorts of correspondences to control gadgets like home machines, mechanical apparatuses, and so on. Comprehensively we can sort them as wired and remote. For instance in remote correspondence we transmit sign utilizing radio recurrence (RF) and in wired correspondence we use wires. Wired correspondence can further be classified as:

- Parallel correspondence

- Sequential Communication

In parallel correspondence we utilize numerous wires relying upon the information size in bits, for example in the event that we have to transmit 8 piece, at that point we would require a 8-piece wire. In any case, in sequential correspondence we just utilized two wires for transmitting information and getting information as in sequential correspondence information are transmitted sequentially for example a little bit at a time.

Components Required

- Arduino UNO

- ULN2003

- Serial Cable

- Bulb with holder

- Relay 5 volt

- Bread board

- Connecting wires

- Laptop

- 16x2 LCD

- PVT

- Power supply

Hand-off

We need a hand-off to interface the circuits with higher voltage AC apparatuses like bulb, TV, fan, and so forth. Transfer is a sort of switch which is utilized for electronic to electrical interfacing. Transfers contain a curl and some exchanging contact centers. There are various sorts of transfers, as:

- Single Pole Single Through (SPST).

- Single Pole Double Through (SPDT).

- Twofold Pole single Through (DPST).

- Twofold Pole Double Through (DPDT).

Here we have utilized single post twofold through (SPDT) hand-off. SPDT transfers contain five pins, in which 2 stick for curl and one is for shaft and other two are in particular "Ordinarily Connected" (NC) and "Regularly Open" (NO).

Circuit Diagram and Explanation

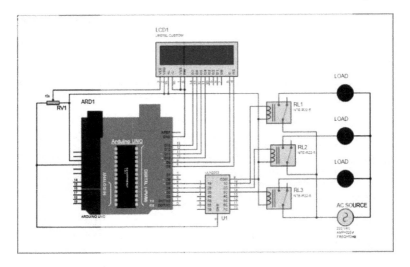

As appeared in the above schematic graph over, a 16x2 LCD module is utilized for showing status of home apparatuses which is straightforwardly associated with arduino in 4-piece mode. Information pins of LCD to be specific RS, EN, D4, D5, D6, D7 are associated with arduino advanced stick number 7, 6, 5, 4, 3, 2. For sending directions to arduino from workstation or PC we utilizes USB link that we utilized for transferring program into arduino. What's more, a transfer driver IC ULN2003 is additionally used for driving transfers. 5 volt SPDT 3 transfers are utilized for controlling LIGHT, FAN as well as TV. Also, transfers are associated with arduino stick number 3, 4 and 5 through hand-off driver IC ULN2003 for controlling LIGHT, FAN and TV individually.

Here sequential correspondence is utilized to manage the home mechanical assemblies. We send directions like LIGHT ON, LIGHT OFF, FAN ON, FAN OFF, TV ON AND TV OFF to control AC home machines. In the wake of getting the given directions, arduino send sign to transfers which are answerable for turning on or off of the machines.

At the point when we press ENTER in the wake of composing one of some random order on hyper terminal or sequential terminal, arduino performs relative undertaking like turning on the "fan" and moreover different ent assignments. Furthermore, a significant message is likewise shown on 16x2 LCD which is modified in the code. (See the code area in base)

Code Explanation

Above all else we incorporate library for fluid precious stone presentation and afterward we characterizes information and control pins for LCD and home machines.

```
#include <LiquidCrystal.h>
LiquidCrystal lcd(13, 12, 11, 10, 9, 8);
#include<string.h>

#define light 3
#define fan 4
#define TV 5
```

After it sequential correspondence is instated at 9600 bps and provides guidance to utilize stick.

```
lcd.begin(16, 2);
Serial.begin(9600);
pinMode(light, OUTPUT);
pinMode(fan, OUTPUT);
pinMode(TV, OUTPUT);
lcd.print(" Home Automation ");
lcd.setCursor(0,1);
```

For accepting information sequentially we utilize two capacities - one is Serial.available which checks any sequential information is coming or not and other one is Serial,read which peruses information that comes sequentially.

```
while(Serial.available())
  {
    char Inchar=Serial.read();
```

In the wake of accepting information sequentially we store it in a string and afterward sit tight for Enter.

```
str[i]=Inchar;
i++;
lcd.print(Inchar);
delay(50);
if(Inchar == 0x0d)
{
  temp=1;
```

When enter is squeezed program begin to contrast got string and right now characterized string and on the off chance that string coordinated, at that point a relative activity is performed by utilizing proper direction that are given in code.

```
if((strncmp(str,"FAN ON", 6))==0)
{
 lcd.clear();
 digitalWrite(fan, HIGH);
```

For utilizing look at string we have utilized a library that is string.h which has a few watchwords like strcmp, strncmp, strcpy and so forth.

Code

```
#include <LiquidCrystal.h>
#include<string.h>
LiquidCrystal lcd(13, 12, 11, 10, 9, 8);
#define light 3
#define fan 4
#define TV 5
char temp;
char str[10];
char i=0;
void setup()
{
 lcd.begin(16, 2);
 Serial.begin(9600);
 pinMode(light, OUTPUT);
 pinMode(fan, OUTPUT);
 pinMode(TV, OUTPUT);
 lcd.print(" Home Automation ");
 lcd.setCursor(0,1);
 lcd.print(" Using PC   ");
 delay(2000);
 lcd.clear();
```

```
lcd.print("Keywords For ");
lcd.setCursor(0,1);
lcd.print("Controlling");
delay(2000);
lcd.clear();
lcd.print("1. LIGHT ON");
lcd.setCursor(0,1);
lcd.print("2. LIGHT OFF");
delay(2000);
lcd.clear();
lcd.print("3. FAN ON");
lcd.setCursor(0,1);
lcd.print("4. FAN OFF");
delay(2000);
lcd.clear();
lcd.print("5. TV ON");
lcd.setCursor(0,1);
lcd.print("6. TV OFF");
delay(2000);
defualt();
delay(1000);
}
void loop()
{
  if(temp==1)
  {
  if((strncmp(str,"FAN ON", 6))==0)
  {
  lcd.clear();
  digitalWrite(fan, HIGH);
```

```
lcd.clear();
lcd.print("Fan Turned On");
delay(3000);
defualt();
}


  else if(strncmp(str, "FAN OFF", 7)==0)
{
digitalWrite(fan, LOW);
lcd.clear();
lcd.print("Fan Turned OFF");
delay(3000);
defualt();
}


  else if(strncmp(str, "LIGHT ON", 8)==0)
{
digitalWrite(light, HIGH);
lcd.clear();
lcd.print("Light Turned ON");
delay(3000);
defualt();
}


  else if(strncmp(str, "LIGHT OFF", 9)==0)
{
digitalWrite(light, LOW);
lcd.clear();
```

```
lcd.print("Light Turned OFF");
delay(3000);
defualt();
}


  else if(strncmp(str, "TV ON", 5)==0)
{
digitalWrite(TV, HIGH);
lcd.clear();
lcd.print("TV Turned ON");
delay(3000);
defualt();
}


  else if(strncmp(str, "TV OFF", 6)==0)
{
digitalWrite(TV, LOW);
lcd.clear();
lcd.print("TV Turned OFF");
delay(3000);
defualt();
}


  else
{
lcd.clear();
lcd.print(" Invalid Input");
lcd.setCursor(0,1);
```

```
  lcd.print(" Try Again ");
  delay(3000);
  defualt();
  }
 }
}
void serialEvent()
{
 while(Serial.available())
 {
  char Inchar=Serial.read();
  str[i]=Inchar;
  i++;
  lcd.print(Inchar);
  delay(50);
  if(Inchar == 0x0d)
  {
  temp=1;
  //Inchar=0;
  }
 }
}
void defualt()
{
 lcd.clear();
 lcd.print("Enter UR Choise:");
 lcd.setCursor(0,1);
 lcd.cursor();
 i=0;
 temp=0;
```

}

❖ ❖ ❖

4. WEIGHT SENSOR BMP180 INTERFACING WITH ARDUINO UNO

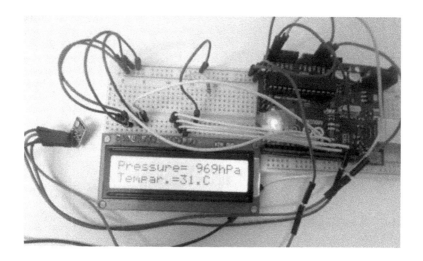

In this instructional exercise we are gonna to structure a Barometric weight Estimating Framework utilizing BMP180 and ARDUINO. As a matter of first importance for interfacing BMP180 to ARDUINO, we have to install a library explicitly intended for BMP180. This library is accessible at: https://github.com/adafruit/Adafruit-BMP085-Library After appending that library, we can call extraordinary capacities which will straightforwardness working with BMP180 sensor.

Components Required

Equipment: Arduino uno board, 220? resistor, interfacing pins, 16x2 LCD, BMP180 Barometric Pressure Sensor, bread board.

Programming: Arduino daily

Circuit Diagram & Working Explanation

In the wake of calling for header we don't have to stress for setting up correspondence between Arduino Uno and BMP180 sensor. We can just bring in uncommon capacities which will do that for us. We just need to Initialize a LCD and show the called qualities from SENSOR on it.

In 16x2 LCD there are 16 sticks over all if there is a backdrop illumination, if there is no backdrop illumination there will be all out 14 pins. One can power or leave the backdrop illumination pins. Presently in the 14 pins there are eight information pins (7-14 or D0-D7), 2 power supply pins (1&2 or VSS&VDD or GND&+5v), third stick for differentiation control (VEE-controls how thick the characters ought to be appeared) as well as three control pins (RS&RW&E).

In the circuit, you can see that I have just took two control sticks, the difference bit and READ/WRITE are not frequently utilized so they can be shorted to ground.

This places LCD in most noteworthy differentiation and read mode. We simply need to control ENABLE and RS pins to send characters and information in like manner.

The associations which are accomplished for LCD are given beneath:

PIN1 or VSS to ground

PIN2 or VDD or VCC to +5v control

PIN3 or VEE to ground (gives most extreme complexity best for a fledgling)

PIN4 or (Register Selection) to PIN8 of ARDUINO UNO

PIN5 or (Read/Write) to ground (places LCD in read mode facilitates the correspondence for client)

PIN6 or (Enable) toPIN9 of ARDUINO UNO

PIN11 or D4 to PIN10 of ARDUINO UNO

PIN12 or D5 to PIN11 of ARDUINO UNO

PIN13 or D6 to PIN12 of ARDUINO UNO

PIN14 or D7 to PIN13 of ARDUINO UNO

The ARDUINO IDE enables the client to utilize LCD in 4 piece mode. This kind of correspondence empowers the client to diminish the stick use on ARDUINO, not at all like other the ARDUINO need not be modified independently for utilizing it in 4 it mode in light of the fact that as a issue of course the ARDUINO is set up to convey in 4 piece mode. In the circuit you can see we have utilized 4 bit correspondence (D4-D7). [Also check: Interface LCD with Arduino Uno]

So from minor perception from above table we are interfacing six pins of LCD to controller in which four pins are information pins and 2 pins for control.

For interfacing the BMP180 to Arduino Uno we have to do following:

1. #include <Adafruit_BMP085.h>
2. #include <Wire.h>
3. #include <LiquidCrystal.h>
4. Serial.begin(9600);
5. String PRESSUREVALUE = String(bmp.readPressure());
6. String TEMPARATUREVALUE = String(bmp.readTemperature());

First we have to call the header document for empowering unique capacities "#include<Adafruit_BMP085.h>".

With this header record we can consider capacities that can peruse values from Sensor legitimately with no fluff.

Presently we have to empower the C correspondence,

this is finished by calling "#include <Wire.h>" header document.

We can peruse pressure by calling" String PRESSURE-VALUE = String(bmp.readPressure());". Here the weight worth will be perused from sensor and is put away in the string "PRESSUREVALUE".

We can peruse temparature by calling" String TEM-PARATUREVALUE = String(bmp.readTemperature());". Here the weight worth will be perused from sensor and is put away in the string "TEMPARATUREVALUE".

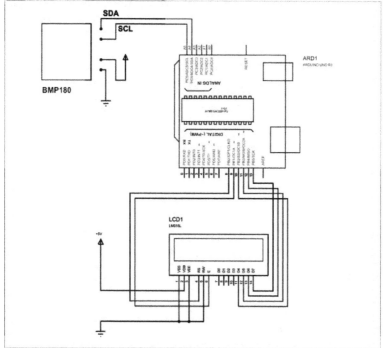

First we have to empower the header document ('#include<LiquidCrystal.h>'), this header record has directions written in it, which empowers the client to interface a LCD to UNO in 4 piece mode with no fluff. With this header document we need not need to send information to LCD a tiny bit at a time, this will all be dealt with as well as we don't have to compose a program for sending information or a direction to LCD a tiny bit at a time.

Second we have to tell the board which sort of LCD we are utilizing here. Since we have such huge numbers of various kinds of LCD (like 20*4, 16*2, 16*1 and so on.). In here we are going to interface a 16*2 LCD to the UNO so we get 'lcd.begin(16,2);'. For 16*1 we get 'lcd.begin(16,1);'.

In this guidance we are gonna to tell the board where we associated the pins, The pins which are associated are to be spoken to all together as "RS, En, D4, D5, D6, D7". These pins are to be spoken to accurately. Since we associated RS to PIN0, etc as show in circuit graph, We speak to the stick number to board as "LiquidCrystallcd(0,1,8,9,10,11);".

After above there all there is left is to send information, the information which should be shown in LCD ought to be composed as "cd.print("hello, world!");". With this order the LCD shows 'hi, world!'.

As should be obvious we need not stress over any this else, we simply have to introduce and the UNO will be prepared to show information. We don't have to compose a program circle to send the information BYTE by BYTE here. In the wake of perusing the incentive from sensor we are going to show them on 16x2 LCD.

Code

```
#include <Adafruit_BMP085.h>
#include <Wire.h>
#include <LiquidCrystal.h>
// initialize the library with the numbers of the interface pins
LiquidCrystal lcd(8, 9, 10, 11, 12, 13);// RS,EN,D4,D5,D6,D7
char PRESSURESHOW[4];// initializing a character of size 4 for showing the result
char TEMPARATURESHOW[4];// initializing a character of size 4 for showing the temparature result
Adafruit_BMP085 bmp;
void setup() {
    lcd.begin(16, 2);
    // Print a logo message to the LCD.
    lcd.print(" HELLOWORLD");
    lcd.setCursor(0, 1);
    delay (2500);
    delay (2500);
```

```
lcd.clear();//clear display
// Print another message to the LCd
Serial.begin(9600);
if(!bmp.begin())
{
      Serial.println("ERROR");///if there is an error
in communication
      while (1) {}
}
}
void loop()
{
      lcd.print("Pressure= ");     // print name
      String PRESSUREVALUE = String(bmp.readPres-
sure());
      // convert the reading to a char array
      PRESSUREVALUE.toCharArray(PRESSURESHOW,
4);
      lcd.print(PRESSURESHOW);
      lcd.print("hPa ");
      lcd.setCursor(0, 1);
      //// set the cursor to column 0, line 1
      lcd.print("Tempar.=");// print name
      String TEMPARATUREVALUE = String(bmp.read-
Temperature());
      // convert the reading to a char array
      TEMPARATUREVALUE.toCharArray(TEMPAR-
```

ANBAZHAGAN K

```
ATURESHOW, 4);
    lcd.print(TEMPARATURESHOW);
    lcd.print("C ");
     lcd.setCursor(0, 0);/ set the cursor to column 0,
line1
    delay(1000);
}
```

◆ ◆ ◆

5. TACHOMETER UTILIZING ARDUINO

Tachometer is a RPM counter which checks the no. of pivot every moment. There are two sorts of tachometer one mechanical as well as other one is advanced. Here we are going to structure an Arduino based computerized tachometer utilizing IR sensor module to distinguish object for check revolution of any turning body. As IR transmits IR beams which reflect back to IR beneficiary and afterward IR Module produces a yield or heartbeat which is recognized by the arduino controller when we press start button. It checks ceaselessly for 5 seconds.

Following 5 seconds arduino ascertain RPM for brief utilizing given equation.

RPM= Count x 12 for single item turning body.

Be that as it may, here we show this task utilizing roof fan. So we have done a few changes that is given underneath:

RPM=count x 12/objects

Where

object = number of sharp edge in fan.

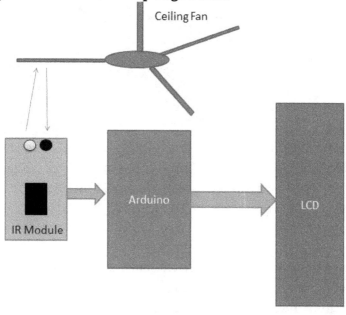

Ceiling Fan

IR Module

Arduino

LCD

Components Used

- Arduino
- 16x2 LCD
- IR sensor Module
- Bread board
- Push button
- Connecting wires
- 9 volt battery

Circuit Diagram and Explanation

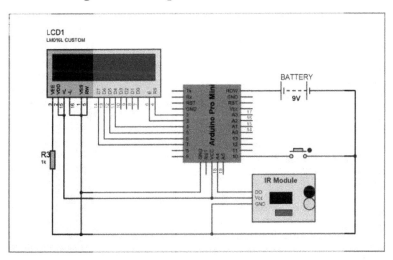

As appeared in the above tachometer circuit, it contains Arduino Pro Mini, IR sensor module, signal and LCD. Arduino controls the entire the procedure like perusing beat that IR sensor module produce as indicated by object location, ascertaining RPM and sending

RPM incentive to LCD. IR sensor is utilized for detecting object. We can set affectability of this sensor module by inbuilt potentiometer arranged on IR module. IR sensor module comprise an IR transmitter as well as a photograph diode which recognizes or gets infrared beams. IR transmitter transmits infrared beams, when these beams fall on any surface, they reflect back and detected by photograph diode (You can see progressively about it in this Line Folloewr Robot). The yield of photograph diode is associated with a comparator, which contrast photograph diode yield and reference voltage and result is given as yield to arduino.

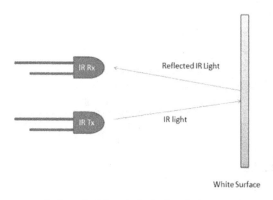

White Surface

IR sensor module yield stick is legitimately associated with stick 18 (A4). Vcc and GND are associated with Vcc and GND of arduino. A 16x2 LCD is associated with arduino in 4-piece mode. Control stick RS, RW and En are legitimately associated with arduino stick 2, GND and 3. Also, information stick D4-D7 is associated with pins 4, 5, 6 and 7 of arduino. A push catch is additionally included this undertaking. At the point when we have to tally RPM we press this catch to begin this Arduino Tachometer to check RPM for five seconds. This push catch is associated with stick 10 of arduino concerning ground.

Program Description

In code we have utilized computerized perused capacity to peruse yield of IR sensor module and afterward figure RPM.

```
int i,j;
unsigned int count=0;
for(i=0;i<1000;i++)
{
  for(j=0;j<1227;j++)
  {
    if(digitalRead(sensor))
    {
      count++;
      while(digitalRead(sensor));
```

Code

```
#include <LiquidCrystal.h>
LiquidCrystal lcd(3, 2, 4, 5, 6, 7);
#define sensor 18
#define start 10
int delay1()
{
 //unsigned int long k;
  int i,j;
  unsigned int count=0;
  for(i=0;i<1000;i++)
  {
```

```
for(j=0;j<1227;j++)
{
if(digitalRead(sensor))
{
 count++;
 while(digitalRead(sensor));
}
}
}
 return count;
}
void setup()
{
 pinMode(sensor, INPUT);
 pinMode(start, INPUT);
 pinMode(13, OUTPUT);
 lcd.begin(16, 2);
 lcd.print("Techometer");
 lcd.setCursor(0,1);
 lcd.print("Hello world");
 delay(2000);
 digitalWrite(start, HIGH);
}
void loop()
{
  unsigned int time=0,RPM=0;
  lcd.clear();
  lcd.print(" Please Press ");
  lcd.setCursor(0,1);
  lcd.print("Button to Start ");
```

```
    while(digitalRead(start));
    lcd.clear();
    lcd.print("Reading RPM.....");
    time=delay1();
    lcd.clear();
    lcd.print("Please Wait.....");
    RPM=(time*12)/3;
    delay(2000);
    lcd.clear();
    lcd.print("RPM=");
    lcd.print(RPM);
    delay(5000);
}
```

❖ ❖ ❖

6. ADVANCED CODE LOCK UTILIZING ARDUINO

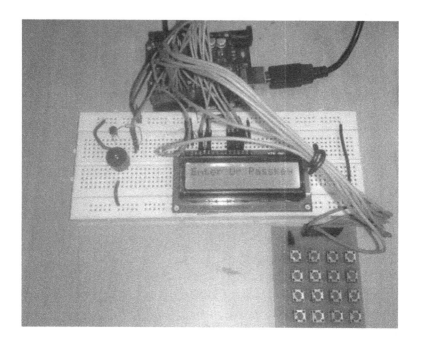

Security is a significant worry in our regular day to day existence, and advanced locks have turned into a significant piece of these security frameworks. One such computerized code lock is imitated in this undertaking utilizing arduino board and a grid keypad.

Components

- Arduino
- Buzzer
- Keypad Module
- BC547 Transistor
- 16x2 LCD
- Bread board
- Resistor (1k)
- Connecting wires
- Power

In this circuit we have utilized multiplexing method to interface keypad for input the secret word in the framework. Here we are utilizing 4x4 keypad which contains 16 key. In the event that we need to utilize 16 keys, at that point we need 16 stick for association with arduino yet in multiplexing strategy we have to utilize just 8 stick for interfacing 16 keys. With the goal that it is a brilliant method to interface a keypad module. [Also check: Keypad Interfacing with Arduino]

Multiplexing Technique: Multiplexing strategy is an extremely proficient approach to diminish number of pins utilized with the microcontroller for giving info or secret key or numbers. Fundamentally this method is utilized in two different ways - one is column filtering and other one is colon checking. Be that as it may, in this arduino based undertaking we have utilized keypad library so we don't have to make any multiplexing code for this framework. We just need to utilize keypad library for giving info.

Circuit Description

Circuit of this undertaking is straightforward which contains Arduino, keypad module, bell and LCD. Arduino controls the total procedures like taking secret key structure keypad module, contrasting passwords, driving signal and sending status to LCD show. Keypad is utilized for taking secret phrase. Signal is utilized for signs and LCD is utilized for showing status or messages on it. Signal is driven by utilizing a NPN transistor.

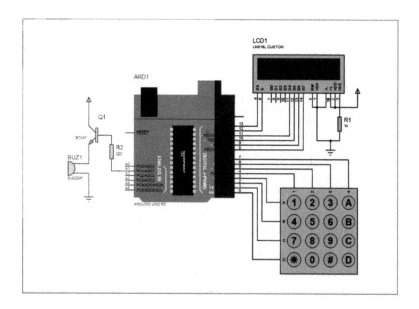

Keypad module's Column pins are legitimately associated with stick 4, 5, 6, 7 and Row pins are associated with 3, 2, 1, 0 of arduino uno. A 16x2 LCD is associated with arduino in 4-piece mode. Control stick RS, RW and En are straightforwardly associated with arduino stick 13, GND and 12. What's more, information stick D4-D7 is associated with pins 11, 10, 9 and 8 of arduino. Furthermore, one signal is associated at stick 14(A1) of arduino through a BC547 NPN transistor.

Working

We have utilized inbuilt arduino's EEPROM to spare secret key, so when we run this circuit first time program read a trash information from inbuilt arduino's EEPROM and contrast it and information secret key and give a message on LCD that is Access Denied on the grounds that secret key doesn't coordinate. For taking care of this issue we have to set a default secret word just because by utilizing programming given underneath:

```
for(int j=0;j<4;j++)

EEPROM.write(j, j+49);
```

```
lcd.print("Enter Ur Passkey:");

lcd.setCursor(0,1);
```

```
for(int j=0;j<4;j++)

pass[j]=EEPROM.read(j);
```

This will set secret key "1234" to EEPROM of Arduino.

Subsequent to running it first time we have to expel this from program and again compose the code in to the arduino and run. Presently your framework will run fine. Also, for your subsequent time utilized secret word is currently "1234". Presently you can transform it by squeezing # catch and afterward enter your present secret word and afterward enter your new secret word.

At the point when you will enter your secret word, framework will contrast your entered secret phrase and that secret key that is put away in EEPROM of arduino. In the event that match is happened, at that point LCD will show "get to allowed" and in the event that secret key isn't right, at that point LCD will "Access Denied" and signal persistently blare for quite a while. Furthermore, ringer is additionally blare a solitary time at whatever point client will press any fasten from keypad.

Programming Description

In code we have utilized keypad library for interfacing keypad with arduino.

```
#include <Keypad.h>

#include<LiquidCrystal.h>

#include<EEPROM.h>
```

```
const byte ROWS = 4; //four rows

const byte COLS = 4; //four columns

char hexaKeys[ROWS][COLS] = {

 {'1','2','3','A'},

 {'4','5','6','B'},

 {'7','8','9','C'},

 {'*','0','#','D'}

};

byte rowPins[ROWS] = {3, 2, 1, 0}; //connect to the
row pinouts of the keypad

byte colPins[COLS] = {4, 5, 6, 7}; //connect to the col-
```

```
umn pinouts of the keypad

//initialize an instance of class NewKeypad

Keypad              customKeypad              =
Keypad( makeKeymap(hexaKeys), rowPins, colPins,
ROWS, COLS);
```

We have included LCD library for LCD interfacing and for interfacing EEPROM we have included library EEPROM.h., and afterward introduced variable and characterized pins for segments.

```
#define buzzer 15

LiquidCrystal lcd(13,12,11,10,9,8);

char password[4];

char pass[4],pass1[4];

int i=0;

char customKey=0;
```

And afterward we instated LCD and provide guidance to pins in arrangement work

```
void setup()

{

  lcd.begin(16,2);

  pinMode(led, OUTPUT);

  pinMode(buzzer, OUTPUT);

  pinMode(m11, OUTPUT);

  pinMode(m12, OUTPUT);

  lcd.print(" Electronic ");

  lcd.setCursor(0,1);

  lcd.print(" Keypad Lock ");

  delay(2000);

  lcd.clear();

  lcd.print("Enter Ur Passkey:");

  lcd.setCursor(0,1);
```

After this we read keypad in circle work

```
customKey = customKeypad.getKey();

  if(customKey=='#')

  change();

  if(customKey)

  {

    password[i++]=customKey;

    lcd.print(customKey);

    beep();

  }
```

And afterward contrast secret phrase and spare secret phrase utilizing string analyze technique.

```
if(i==4)

  {

    delay(200);
```

```
for(int j=0;j<4;j++)

pass[j]=EEPROM.read(j);

if(!(strncmp(password, pass,4)))

{

   digitalWrite(led, HIGH);

   beep();

   lcd.clear();

   lcd.print("Passkey Accepted");

   delay(2000);

   lcd.setCursor(0,1);

   lcd.print("#.Change Passkey");

   delay(2000);

   lcd.clear();

   lcd.print("Enter Passkey:");

   lcd.setCursor(0,1);
```

```
    i=0;

    digitalWrite(led, LOW);

}
```

This is secret key change capacity and ringer blare work

```
void change()

{

int j=0;

lcd.clear();

lcd.print("UR Current Passk");

lcd.setCursor(0,1);

while(j<4)

{

 char key=customKeypad.getKey();

 if(key)
```

```
  {

    pass1[j++]=key;

    lcd.print(key);

  void beep()

  {

    digitalWrite(buzzer, HIGH);

    delay(20);

    digitalWrite(buzzer, LOW);

  }
```

Code

```
#include <Keypad.h>
#include<LiquidCrystal.h>
#include<EEPROM.h>
#define buzzer 15
LiquidCrystal lcd(13,12,11,10,9,8);
char password[4];
char pass[4],pass1[4];
int i=0;
char customKey=0;
const byte ROWS = 4; //four rows
```

```
const byte COLS = 4; //four columns
char hexaKeys[ROWS][COLS] = {
 {'1','2','3','A'},
 {'4','5','6','B'},
 {'7','8','9','C'},
 {'*','0','#','D'}
};
byte rowPins[ROWS] = {3, 2, 1, 0}; //connect to the row
pinouts of the keypad
byte colPins[COLS] = {4, 5, 6, 7}; //connect to the col-
umn pinouts of the keypad
//initialize an instance of class NewKeypad
Keypad              customKeypad              =
Keypad( makeKeymap(hexaKeys), rowPins, colPins,
ROWS, COLS);
void setup()
{
 lcd.begin(16,2);
 pinMode(led, OUTPUT);
 pinMode(buzzer, OUTPUT);
 pinMode(m11, OUTPUT);
 pinMode(m12, OUTPUT);
 lcd.print(" Electronic ");
 lcd.setCursor(0,1);
 lcd.print(" Keypad Lock ");
 delay(2000);
 lcd.clear();
 lcd.print("Enter Ur Passkey:");
 lcd.setCursor(0,1);
 for(int j=0;j<4;j++)
```

```
EEPROM.write(j, j+49);
for(int j=0;j<4;j++)
pass[j]=EEPROM.read(j);
}


void loop()
{
customKey = customKeypad.getKey();
if(customKey=='#')
change();
if(customKey)
{
  password[i++]=customKey;
  lcd.print(customKey);
  beep();
}
if(i==4)
{
 delay(200);
 for(int j=0;j<4;j++)
 pass[j]=EEPROM.read(j);
 if(!(strncmp(password, pass,4)))
 {
  digitalWrite(led, HIGH);
  beep();
  lcd.clear();
  lcd.print("Passkey Accepted");
  delay(2000);
  lcd.setCursor(0,1);
  lcd.print("#.Change Passkey");
```

```
    delay(2000);
    lcd.clear();
    lcd.print("Enter Passkey:");
    lcd.setCursor(0,1);
    i=0;
    digitalWrite(led, LOW);
  }


    else
  {
   digitalWrite(buzzer, HIGH);
   lcd.clear();
   lcd.print("Access Denied...");
   lcd.setCursor(0,1);
   lcd.print("#.Change Passkey");
   delay(2000);
   lcd.clear();
   lcd.print("Enter Passkey:");
   lcd.setCursor(0,1);
   i=0;
   digitalWrite(buzzer, LOW);
  }
 }
}
void change()
{
 int j=0;
 lcd.clear();
 lcd.print("UR Current Passk");
 lcd.setCursor(0,1);
```

```
while(j<4)
{
 char key=customKeypad.getKey();
 if(key)
 {
  pass1[j++]=key;
  lcd.print(key);
  beep();
 }
 key=0;
}
delay(500);


 if((strncmp(pass1, pass, 4)))
{
 lcd.clear();
 lcd.print("Wrong Passkey...");
 lcd.setCursor(0,1);
 lcd.print("Better Luck Again");
 delay(1000);
}
else
{
 j=0;

 lcd.clear();
lcd.print("Enter New Passk:");
lcd.setCursor(0,1);
while(j<4)
```

```
{
 char key=customKeypad.getKey();
 if(key)
 {
  pass[j]=key;
  lcd.print(key);
  EEPROM.write(j,key);
  j++;
  beep();
 }
}
lcd.print(" Done......");
delay(1000);
}
lcd.clear();
lcd.print("Enter Ur Passk:");
lcd.setCursor(0,1);
customKey=0;
}
void beep()
{
 digitalWrite(buzzer, HIGH);
 delay(20);
 digitalWrite(buzzer, LOW);
}
```

◆ ◆ ◆

7. SHADING DETECTOR UTILIZING ARDUINO UNO

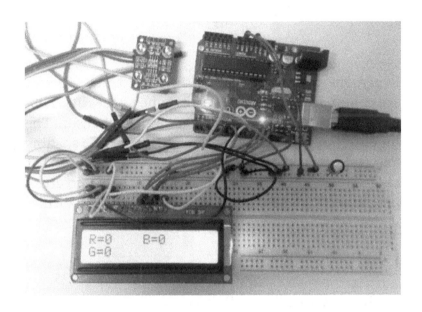

In this task we are going to interface TCS3200 shading sensor with Arduino UNO. TCS3200 is a shading sensor which can identify any number of hues with right programming. TCS3200 contains RGB (Red Green Blue) exhibits. As appeared in figure on minute level one can see the square boxes inside the eye on sensor. These square boxes are varieties of RGB grid. Each of these cases contain Three sensors, One is for detecting RED light power, One is for detecting GREEN light force and the rearward in for detecting BLUE light force.

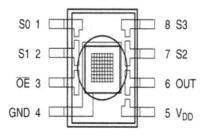

Every one of sensor exhibits in these three clusters are chosen independently relying upon necessity. Subsequently it is known as programmable sensor. The module can be included to detect the specific shading and to leave the others. It contains channels for that choice reason. There is forward mode that is no channel mode. With no channel mode the sensor identifies white light.

Components Required

Equipment: ARDUINO UNO, control supply (5v), LED, JHD_162ALCD (16*2LCD),TCS3200 shading sensor.

Programming: ARDUINO IDE (ARDUINO daily).

Circuit Diagram and Working Explanation

In 16x2 LCD there are 16 sticks over all if there is a backdrop illumination, if there is no backdrop illumination there will be 14 pins. One can power or leave the backdrop illumination pins. Presently in the 14 pins there are 8 information pins (7-14 or D0-D7), 2 power supply pins (1&2 or VSS&VDD or GND&+5v), third stick for difference control (VEE-controls how thick the characters ought to be appeared), as well as three control pins (RS&RW&E)

In the circuit, you can watch I have just took two control pins. The complexity bit and READ/WRITE are not frequently utilized so they can be shorted to ground. This places LCD in most noteworthy differentiation and read mode. We simply have to manage ENABLE as well as RS pins to send characters as well as information in like manner. [Also check: LCD interfacing with Arduino Uno]

The associations which are accomplished for LCD are given beneath:

PIN1 or VSS to ground

PIN2 or VDD or VCC to +5v control

PIN3 or VEE to ground (gives greatest complexity best for a fledgling)

PIN4 or (Register Selection) to PIN8 of ARDUINO UNO

PIN5 or (Read/Write) to ground (places LCD in read mode facilitates the correspondence for client)

PIN6 or (Enable) to PIN9 of ARDUINO UNO

PIN11 or D4 to PIN7 of ARDUINO UNO

PIN12 or D5 to PIN11 of ARDUINO UNO

PIN13 or D6 to PIN12 of ARDUINO UNO

PIN14 or D7 to PIN13 of ARDUINO UNO

The associations which are accomplished for shading sensor are given beneath:

VDD to +5V

GND to GROUND

OE (yield Enable) to GND

S0 to UNO stick 2

S1 to UNO stick 3

S2 to UNO stick 4

S3 to UNO stick 5

OUT to UNO stick 10

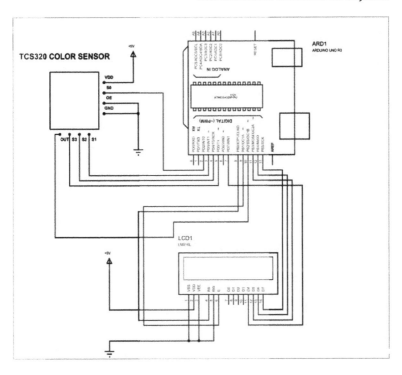

The shading which should be detected by the shading sensor is chosen by two pins S2 as well as S3. With these two pins rationale control we can tell sensor which shading light power is to be estimated.

Let's assume we have to detect the RED shading force we have to set the two pins to LOW. When that is done the sensor identifies the force and sends the incentive to the control framework inside the module.

S2	S3	Photodiode Type

L	L	Red
L	H	Blue
H	L	Clear (no filter)
H	H	Green

The control framework inside the module is appeared in figure. The light power estimated by exhibit is sent to current to recurrence converter. What it does is, it puts out a square wave whose recurrence is in connection to current sent by ARRAY.

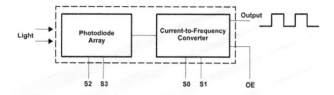

So we have a framework which conveys a square wave whose recurrence relies upon light power of shading which is chosen by S2 and S3.

The sign recurrence sent by module can be balanced relying upon use. We can change the yield signal recurrence data transmission.

S0	S1	Output Frequency Scaling (f_o)
L	L	Power Down

L	H	2%
H	L	20%
H	H	100%

The recurrence scaling is finished by two bits S0 and S1. For accommodation we are going to constrain the recurrence scaling to 20%. This is finished by setting S0 to high and S1 to LOW. This component proves to be useful when we are utilizing the module on framework with low clock.

The Array affectability to shading is appeared in underneath figure.

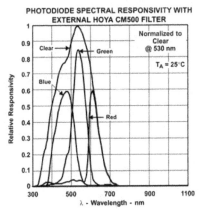

Albeit various hues have distinctive affectability, for an ordinary use it won't have a lot of effect.

The UNO here send sign to module to identify hues and the information got by the module is appeared in the

16*2 LCD associated with it.

The UNO distinguishes three shading forces independently and shows them on LCD.

The Uno can identify the sign heartbeat length by which we can get the recurrence of square wave sent by module. With the current recurrence we can coordinate it with shading on sensor.

```
Int frequency = pulseIn(10, LOW);
```

As by above condition the UNO peruses beat term on tenth stick of UNO and stores it esteem in "recurrence" number.

We will do this for all of the three hues for shading acknowledgment. Each of the three shading powers are appeared by frequencies on 16x2 LCD.

Code

```
int OutPut = 10;//naming pin10 of uno as output
unsigned int frequency = 0;
#include <LiquidCrystal.h>
// initialize the library with the numbers of the interface pins
LiquidCrystal lcd(8, 9, 7, 11, 12, 13);// RS,EN,D4,D5,D6,D7
void setup()
```

```
{
    // set up the LCD's number of columns and rows
    lcd.begin(16, 2);
    pinMode(2, OUTPUT);
    pinMode(3, OUTPUT);//PINS 2, 3,4,5 as OUTPUT
    pinMode(4, OUTPUT);
    pinMode(5, OUTPUT);
    pinMode(10, INPUT);//PIN 10 as input
    digitalWrite(2,HIGH);
    digitalWrite(3,LOW);//setting frequency selection to 20%
}
void loop()
{
    lcd.print("R=");//printing name
    digitalWrite(4,LOW);
        digitalWrite(5,LOW);//setting for RED color sensor
        frequency = pulseIn(OutPut, LOW);//reading frequency
            lcd.print(frequency);//printing RED color frequency
    lcd.print(" ");
    lcd.setCursor(7,0);//moving courser to position 7
    delay(500);
    lcd.print("B=");// printing name
    digitalWrite(4,LOW);
```

```
        digitalWrite(5,HIGH);// setting for BLUE color
sensor
        frequency = pulseIn(OutPut, LOW);// reading
frequency
        lcd.print(frequency);// printing BLUE color
frequency
    lcd.print(" ");
    lcd.setCursor(0, 1);
    delay(500);
    lcd.print("G=");// printing name
    digitalWrite(4,HIGH);
    digitalWrite(5,HIGH);// setting for GREEN color
sensor
        frequency = pulseIn(OutPut, LOW);// reading
frequency
        lcd.print(frequency);// printing GREEN color
frequency
    lcd.print(" ");
    lcd.setCursor(0, 0);
    delay(500);
}
```

❖ ❖ ❖

8. PROGRAMMED ROOM LIGHT CONTROLLER WITH BIDIRECTIONAL VISITOR COUNTER

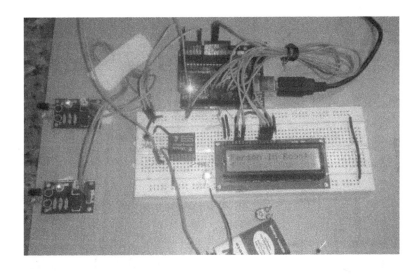

Frequently we see guest counters at arena, shopping center, workplaces, homerooms and so on. How they check the individuals and turn ON or OFF the light when no one is inside? Today we are here with programmed room light controller venture with bidirectional guest counter by utilizing Arduino Uno. It is extremely fascinating undertaking for specialists and understudies for entertainment just as learning.

Components

- Arduino UNO
- Resisters
- Relay (5v)
- 16x2 LCD display
- IR Sensor module
- Connecting Wires
- Bread Board
- BC547 Transistor
- Led

The undertaking of "Computerized guest counter" depends on the interfacing of certain parts, for example, sensors, engines and so forth with arduino microcontroller. This counter can include individuals in the 2 bearings. This circuit can be utilized to check the quantity of people entering a lobby/shopping center/home/office in the passageway entryway and it can tally the quantity of people leaving the corridor by decrementing the tally at same door or leave door and it relies on sensor situation in shopping center/lobby. It can likewise be utilized at doors of stopping regions and other open spots.

This task is separated in four sections: sensors, controller, counter show and door. The sensor would watch an interference and give a contribution to the controller which would run the counter augmentation or decrement relying upon entering or leaving of the individual. What's more, checking is shown on a 16x2 LCD through the controller.

At the point when any one goes into in the room, IR sensor will get hindered by the item then other sensor won't work since we have included a deferral for some time.

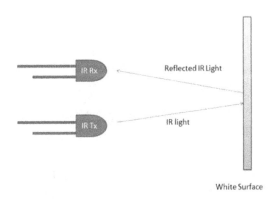

White Surface

Circuit Explanation

There are a few segments of entire guest counter circuit that are sensor area, control segment, show segment and driver segment.

Sensor segment: In this area we have utilized 2 IR sensor modules which contain IR diodes, potentiometer, Comparator (Op-Amp) and LED's. Potentiometer is utilized for setting reference voltage at comparator's one terminal as well as IR sensors sense the item or individual and give an adjustment in voltage at comparator's subsequent terminal. At that point comparator looks at the two voltages and creates an advanced sign at yield. Here in this circuit we have utilized two comparators for two sensors. LM358 is utilized as comparator. LM358 has inbuilt two low commotion Op-amp.

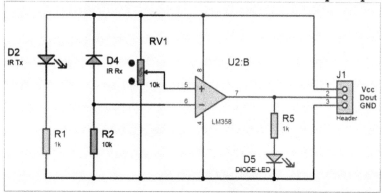

Control Section: Arduino UNO is utilized for controlling entire the procedure of this guest counter undertaking. The yields of comparators are associated with computerized stick number 14 and 19 of arduino. Arduino read these sign and send directions to hand-off driver circuit to drive the transfer for light controlling. In case you discover any trouble in working with transfer, look at this instructional exercise on arduino hand-off control to get familiar with working hand-off with Arduino.

Show segment: Display segment contains a 16x2 LCD. This area will show the checked number of individuals and light status when nobody will in the room.

Transfer Driver segment: Relay driver segment comprise a BC547 transistor and a 5 volt hand-off for controlling the light. Transistor is utilized to drive the transfer in light of the fact that arduino doesn't supply enough voltage as well as current to drive hand-off. So we included a hand-off driver circuit to get enough voltage as well as momentum for hand-off. Arduino sends directions to this hand-off driver transistor and afterward light will turn on/off in like manner.

Visitor Counter Circuit Diagram

The yields of IR Sensor Modules are straightforwardly associated with arduino computerized stick number 14(A0) and 19(A5). What's more, Relay driver transistor at advanced stick 2. LCD is associated in 4 piece mode. RS and EN stick of LCD is legitimately associated at 13 and 12. Information stick of LCD D4-D7 is additionally legitimately associated with arduino at D11-D8 individually. Rest of associations are appeared in the beneath circuit graph.

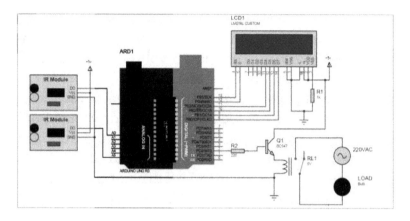

Code Explanation

First we have included library for LCD and character-ized stick for the equivalent. And furthermore characterized information yield stick for sensors and ralay.

```
#include<LiquidCrystal.h>
LiquidCrystal lcd(13,12,11,10,9,8);

#define in 14
#define out 19
#define relay 2
```

At that point provided guidance to information yield stick and introduced LCD in arrangement circle.

```
void setup()
{
  lcd.begin(16,2);
  lcd.print("Visitor Counter");
  delay(2000);
  pinMode(in, INPUT);
  pinMode(out, INPUT);
  pinMode(relay, OUTPUT);
  lcd.clear();
  lcd.print("Person In Room:");
  lcd.setCursor(0,1);
```

In circle work we read sensors info and augmentation or decrement the checking relying on enter or leave activity. And furthermore check for zero condition. Zero condition implies nobody in the room. In the event that zero condition is valid, at that point arduino mood killer the bulb by deactivating the hand-off through transistor.

```
void loop()
{

  if(digitalRead(in))
  IN();
  if(digitalRead(out))
  OUT();

  if(count<=0)
  {
    lcd.clear();
    digitalWrite(relay, LOW);
    lcd.clear();
    lcd.print("No Body In Room");
    lcd.setCursor(0,1);
```

Furthermore, in the event that zero condition is false, at that point arduino turns on the light. Here is two capacities for enter and exit.

```
void IN()                          void OUT()
{                                  {
    count++;                          count--;
    lcd.clear();                      lcd.clear();
    lcd.print("Person In Room:");     lcd.print("Person In Room:");
    lcd.setCursor(0,1);               lcd.setCursor(0,1);
    lcd.print(count);                 lcd.print(count);
    delay(1000);                      delay(1000);
```

Code

```
#include<LiquidCrystal.h>
LiquidCrystal lcd(13,12,11,10,9,8);
#define in 14
#define out 19
#define relay 2
int count=0;
void IN()
{
  count++;
  lcd.clear();
  lcd.print("Person In Room:");
  lcd.setCursor(0,1);
  lcd.print(count);
  delay(1000);
}
void OUT()
```

```
{
 count--;
  lcd.clear();
  lcd.print("Person In Room:");
  lcd.setCursor(0,1);
  lcd.print(count);
  delay(1000);
}
void setup()
{
 lcd.begin(16,2);
 lcd.print("Visitor Counter");
 delay(2000);
 pinMode(in, INPUT);
 pinMode(out, INPUT);
 pinMode(relay, OUTPUT);
 lcd.clear();
 lcd.print("Person In Room:");
 lcd.setCursor(0,1);
 lcd.print(count);
}
void loop()
{


  if(digitalRead(in))
 IN();
 if(digitalRead(out))
 OUT();
```

```
if(count<=0)
{
lcd.clear();
digitalWrite(relay, LOW);
lcd.clear();
lcd.print("Nobody In Room");
lcd.setCursor(0,1);
lcd.print("Light Is Off");
delay(200);
}


else
digitalWrite(relay, HIGH);


}
```

◆ ◆ ◆

9. ELECTRONIC VOTING MACHINE UTILIZING ARDUINO

We as a whole are very acquainted with casting a ballot machines, even we have secured hardly any other electronic democratic machine extends beforehand here and here utilizing RFID and AVR microcontroller. In this task, we have utilized the arduino controller to make an electronic democratic machine.

Components

- Arduino Uno
- Push button
- 16x2 LCD
- Power
- Bread board
- Connecting wires

Circuit Diagram and Working Explanation

In this undertaking we have utilized four push catches for four unique competitors. We can expand the quantity of up-and-comer however for better understanding we have restricted it to four. At the point when any voter press any of four catch at that point regarding casting a ballot worth will augment by one each time. After entire casting a ballot we will press result catch to see the outcomes. As the "result" button is squeezed, arduino computes the all out votes of every up-and-comer and show it on LCD show.

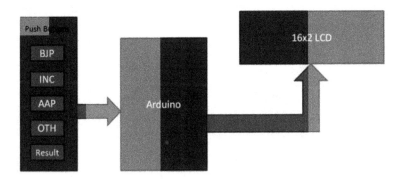

Circuit of this task is very simple which contains Arduino, push catches and LCD. Arduino controls the total procedures like understanding catch, augmenting vote esteem, creating result and sending vote and result to LCD. Here we have included five fastens in which first catch is for BJP, second for INC, third is for AAP, forward is for OTH implies others and last catch is utilized for ascertaining or showing results.

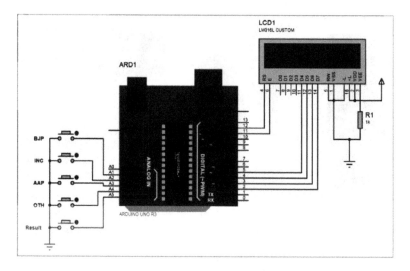

The five push catches are legitimately associated with stick 15-19(A1-A5) of Arduino as for ground. A 16x2 LCD is associated with arduino in 4-piece mode. Control stick RS, RW and En are straightforwardly associated with arduino stick 12, GND and 11. Also, information stick D4-D7 is associated with pins 5, 4, 3 as well as 2 of arduino.

Program Description

Above all else we incorporate header and characterize pins for LCD and than introduce a few factors and stick for taking applicant's democratic information means switch.

```
#include<LiquidCrystal.h>
LiquidCrystal lcd(12, 11, 5, 4, 3, 2);

#define sw1 15
#define sw2 16
#define sw3 17
#define sw4 18
#define sw5 19
int vote1=0;
int vote2=0;
int vote3=0;
int vote4=0;
```

After it, introduce the LCD and provide guidance to include yield pins.

```
void setup()
{
  pinMode(sw1, INPUT);
  pinMode(sw2,INPUT);
  pinMode(sw3,INPUT);
  pinMode(sw4,INPUT);
  pinMode(sw5,INPUT);
  lcd.begin(16, 2);
  lcd.print("Voting Machine");
  lcd.setCursor(0,1);
  lcd.print("Circuit Digest");
  delay(3000);
```

and afterward make pullup the information stick by programming.

```
digitalWrite(sw1, HIGH);
digitalWrite(sw2, HIGH);
digitalWrite(sw3, HIGH);
digitalWrite(sw4, HIGH);
digitalWrite(sw5, HIGH);
lcd.clear();
```

In code we have utilized advanced perused capacity to peruse Button squeezed.

```
if(digitalRead(sw1)==0)
  vote1++;
  while(digitalRead(sw1)==0);
if(digitalRead(sw2)==0)
  vote2++;
  while(digitalRead(sw2)==0);
if(digitalRead(sw3)==0)
  vote3++;
  while(digitalRead(sw3)==0);
 if(digitalRead(sw4)==0)
  vote4++;
```

And afterward showing deciding on the LCD with the applicant gathering's Name.

```
lcd.setCursor(0,0);
lcd.print("BJP");
lcd.setCursor(1,1);
lcd.print(vote1);
lcd.setCursor(4,0);
lcd.print("INC");
lcd.setCursor(5,1);
lcd.print(vote2);
lcd.setCursor(8,0);
lcd.print("AAP");
 lcd.setCursor(9,1);
lcd.print(vote3);
lcd.setCursor(12,0);
lcd.print("OTH");
```

Code

```
#include<LiquidCrystal.h>
LiquidCrystal lcd(12, 11, 5, 4, 3, 2);
#define sw1 15
#define sw2 16
#define sw3 17
#define sw4 18
#define sw5 19
int vote1=0;
int vote2=0;
int vote3=0;
int vote4=0;
void setup()
{
 pinMode(sw1, INPUT);
```

```
pinMode(sw2,INPUT);
pinMode(sw3,INPUT);
pinMode(sw4,INPUT);
pinMode(sw5,INPUT);
lcd.begin(16,2);
lcd.print("Voting Machine");
lcd.setCursor(0,1);
lcd.print("Hello world");
delay(3000);
digitalWrite(sw1,HIGH);
digitalWrite(sw2,HIGH);
digitalWrite(sw3,HIGH);
digitalWrite(sw4,HIGH);
digitalWrite(sw5,HIGH);
lcd.clear();
lcd.setCursor(0,0);
lcd.print("BJP");
lcd.setCursor(4,0);
lcd.print("INC");
lcd.setCursor(8,0);
lcd.print("AAP");
lcd.setCursor(12,0);
lcd.print("OTH");
}
void loop()
{
lcd.setCursor(0,0);
lcd.print("BJP");
lcd.setCursor(1,1);
lcd.print(vote1);
```

```
lcd.setCursor(4,0);
lcd.print("INC");
lcd.setCursor(5,1);
lcd.print(vote2);
lcd.setCursor(8,0);
lcd.print("AAP");
lcd.setCursor(9,1);
lcd.print(vote3);
lcd.setCursor(12,0);
lcd.print("OTH");
lcd.setCursor(13,1);
lcd.print(vote4);
if(digitalRead(sw1)==0)
 vote1++;
 while(digitalRead(sw1)==0);
if(digitalRead(sw2)==0)
 vote2++;
 while(digitalRead(sw2)==0);
if(digitalRead(sw3)==0)
 vote3++;
 while(digitalRead(sw3)==0);
if(digitalRead(sw4)==0)
 vote4++;
 while(digitalRead(sw4)==0);
if(digitalRead(sw5)==0)
{
 int vote=vote1+vote2+vote3+vote4;
 if(vote)
 {
    if((vote1 > vote2 && vote1 > vote3 && vote1 >
```

```
vote4))
  {
  lcd.clear();
  lcd.print("BJP Wins");
  delay(2000);
  lcd.clear();
  }
  else if((vote2 > vote1 && vote2 > vote3 && vote2 >
vote4))
  {
  lcd.clear();
  lcd.print("INC Wins");
  delay(2000);
  lcd.clear();
  }
  else if((vote3 > vote1 && vote3 > vote2 && vote3 >
vote4))
  {
  lcd.clear();
  lcd.print("AAP Wins");
  delay(2000);
  lcd.clear();
  }
  else if(vote4 > vote1 && vote4 > vote2 && vote4 >
vote3)
  {
  lcd.setCursor(0,0);
  lcd.clear();
  lcd.print("OTH Wins");
  delay(2000);
```

```
    lcd.clear();
  }


    else if(vote4 > vote1 && vote4 > vote2 && vote4 >
vote3)
  {
  lcd.setCursor(0,0);
  lcd.clear();
  lcd.print("OTH Wins");
  delay(2000);
  lcd.clear();
  }


    else
  {
  lcd.clear();
  lcd.print(" Tie Up Or ");
  lcd.setCursor(0,1);
  lcd.print(" No Result ");
  delay(1000);
  lcd.clear();
  }


  }
  else
  {
  lcd.clear();
  lcd.print("No Voting....");
```

```
  delay(1000);
  lcd.clear();
}
vote1=0;vote2=0;vote3=0;vote4=0,vote=0;
lcd.clear();
}


}
```

❖ ❖ ❖

10. ARDUINO BASED HEARTBEAT MONITOR

Pulse, internal heat level and circulatory strain observing are significant parameters of human body. Specialists utilize different sort of restorative contraption like thermometer for checking fever or internal heat level, BP screen for pulse estimation and pulse screen for pulse estimation. In this task, we have fabricated an Arduino based heartbeat screen which includes the quantity of pulses in a moment. Here we have utilized a heartbeat sensor module which detects the heartbeat after putting a finger on the sensor.

Components

- Arduino
- 16x2 LCD
- Heart Beat sensor module
- Bread board
- Push button
- Connecting wires
- Power

Working of Heartbeat Monitor Project

Working of this task is very simple yet a little computation for ascertaining pulse is required. There are a few techniques for figuring pulse, yet here we have perused just five heartbeats. At that point we have determined absolute heart beat in a moment by applying the beneath equation:

Five_pusle_time=time2-time1;

Single_pulse_time= Five_pusle_time/5;

rate=60000/Single_pulse_time;

where time1 is first heartbeat counter worth

time2 is rundown heartbeat counter worth

rate is last pulse.

At the point when first heartbeat comes, we start counter by utilizing clock counter capacity in arduino that is millis();. Also, take first heartbeat counter worth structure millis();. At that point we sit tight for five heartbeats. Subsequent to getting five beats we again take counter an incentive in time2 and afterward we substarct time1 from time2 to take unique time taken by five beats. And afterward separate this time by multiple times for getting single heartbeat time. Presently we possess energy for single heartbeat and we can without much of a stretch discover the beat in one moment, deviding 600000 ms by single heartbeat time.

Rate= 600000/single heartbeat time.

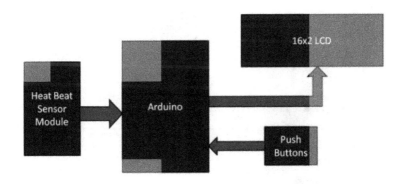

In this task we have utilized Heart beat sensor module

to distinguish Heart Beat. This sensor module contains an IR pair which really distinguish heart beat from blood. Heart siphons the blood in body which is called heart beat, when it happens the blood fixation in body changes. Furthermore, we utilize this change to make a voltage or heartbeat electrically.

Circuit Diagram and Explanation

Circuit of heartbeat screen is demonstrated as follows, which contains arduino uno, heart beat sensor module, reset catch and LCD. Arduino controls entire the procedure of framework like perusing heartbeats structure Heart beat sensor module, figuring pulse and sending this information to LCD. We can set the affectability of this sensor module by inbuilt potentiometer put on this module.

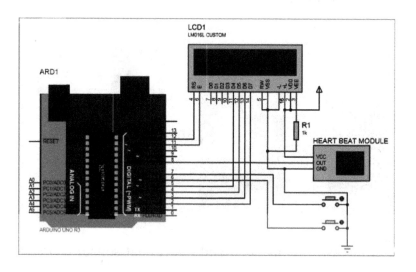

Heart beat sensor module's yield stick is legitimately associated with stick 8 of arduino. Vcc and GND are associated with Vcc and GND. A 16x2 LCD is associated with arduino in 4-piece mode. Control stick RS, RW and En are straightforwardly associated with arduino stick 12, GND and 11. Furthermore, information stick D4-D7 is associated with pins 5, 4, 3 and 2 of arduino. Furthermore, one push catch is included for resetting perusing and another is utilized to begin the framework for understanding heartbeats. At the point when we have to tally pulse, we press start button then arduino start checking heartbeats and furthermore start counter for five seconds. This beginning push catch is associated with stick 7 and reset push catch is associated with stick 6 of arduino as for ground.

Program Description

In code we have utilized advanced perused capacity to peruse yield of Heart Beat sensor module and millis() fuction for figuring time and afterward ascertain Heart Rate.

```
if(!(digitalRead(start)))
{
  k=0;
  lcd.clear();
  lcd.print("Please wait.......");
  while(k<5)
  {
   if(digitalRead(in))
   {
    if(k==0)
    time1=millis();
    k++;
    while(digitalRead(in)):

  time2=millis();
  rate=time2-time1;
  rate=rate/5;
  rate=60000/rate;
  lcd.clear();
  lcd.print("Heart Beat Rate:");
  lcd.setCursor(0,1);
  lcd.print(rate);
  lcd.print(" ");
  lcd.write(1);
```

Before this we have initiazed every one of the parts that we utilized in this task.

```
void setup()
{
  lcd.createChar(1, heart);
  lcd.begin(16,2);

  lcd.print("Heart Beat ");
  lcd.write(1);
  lcd.setCursor(0,1);
  lcd.print("Monitering");
  pinMode(in, INPUT);
  pinMode(Reset, INPUT);
  pinMode(start, INPUT);
```

what's more, here we have pullup the push catch line by utilizing programming pullup.

```
  digitalWrite(Reset, HIGH);
  digitalWrite(start, HIGH);
```

Code

#include<LiquidCrystal.h>

```
LiquidCrystal lcd(12, 11, 5, 4, 3, 2);
int in = 8;
int Reset = 6;
int start = 7;
int count=0,i=0,k=0,rate=0;
unsigned long time2,time1;
unsigned long time;
byte heart[8] =
{
 0b00000,
 0b01010,
 0b11111,
 0b11111,
 0b11111,
 0b01110,
 0b00100,
 0b00000
};
void setup()
{
 lcd.createChar(1, heart);
 lcd.begin(16,2);


  lcd.print("Heart Beat ");
 lcd.write(1);
 lcd.setCursor(0,1);
 lcd.print("Monitering");
 pinMode(in, INPUT);
 pinMode(Reset, INPUT);
```

```
 pinMode(start, INPUT);
 digitalWrite(Reset, HIGH);
 digitalWrite(start, HIGH);
 delay(1000);
}
void loop()
{
 if(!(digitalRead(start)))
 {
  k=0;
  lcd.clear();
  lcd.print("Please wait.......");
  while(k<5)
  {
  if(digitalRead(in))
  {
  if(k==0)
  time1=millis();
  k++;
  while(digitalRead(in));
  }
  }
  time2=millis();
  rate=time2-time1;
  rate=rate/5;
  rate=60000/rate;
  lcd.clear();
  lcd.print("Heart Beat Rate:");
  lcd.setCursor(0,1);
  lcd.print(rate);
```

```
  lcd.print(" ");
  lcd.write(1);
  k=0;
  rate=0;
 }
if(!digitalRead(Reset))
{
 rate=0;
 lcd.clear();
 lcd.print("Heart Beat Rate:");
 lcd.setCursor(0,1);
 lcd.write(1);
 lcd.print(rate);
 k=0;
}
}
```

Thank you !!!